The Vi

Helen Chapman

Illustrated by Bettina Guthridge

PEARSON

Education
Canada

Toronto

Everyone is excited.
A zookeeper is giving a talk at our school today.

We have to figure out the best way to arrange the chairs.
There are 24 students in our class.
Our teacher, Mr. Martin, says, "I wonder how many different ways you can arrange the chairs."

Everyone wants to be in the front row.
We try 1 row of 24 chairs.

Cool! No one is in front of us.
But the students at each end grumble.
"We're squashed against the wall."
Let's try something else.

1 × 24

Jacques says, "Let's try 2 rows of 12 chairs."

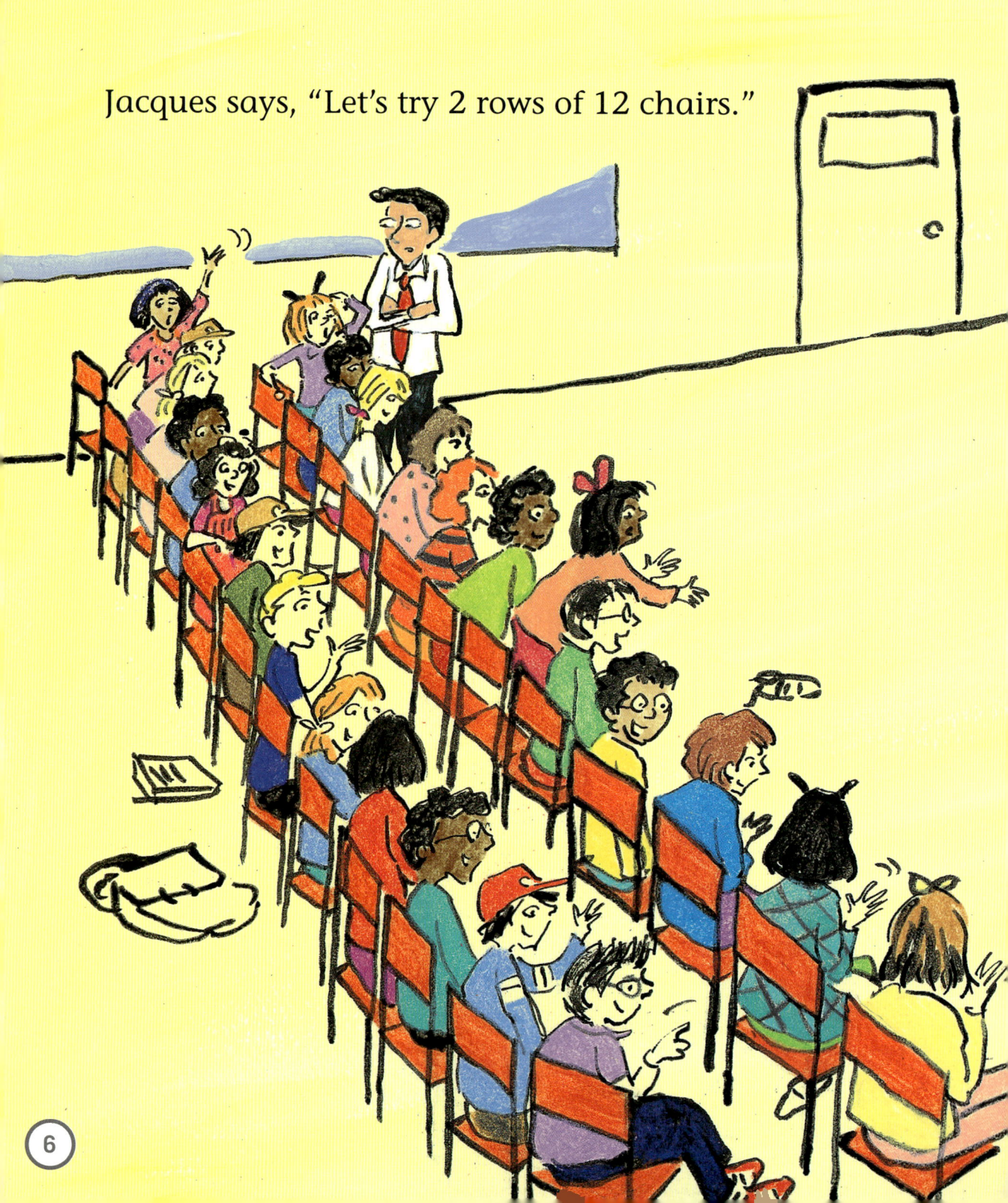

The zookeeper is holding up a wriggling sack.
We cannot see what is inside.
Some students move to get a closer look.

2 × 12

Stella says, "Let's try 3 rows of 8."

Ah, cute!

It is a baby owl.

If we get closer, the zookeeper might let us pat it.

3 × 8

Li says, "Let's try 4 rows of 6."
Oh, the zookeeper has put the owl away.
But look!
She is bringing out a llama.
Let's go all the way to the front.

4 × 6

Claire says, "Let's try 6 rows of 4."
The llama curls its lip and spits.
We are soaked.
"This is fun," say some of the students.
"No, it's not," say the rest. "We're moving back."

6 × 4

Pablo says, "Let's try 8 rows of 3."
Some students squeal. "The floor is wet!"
Let's try something else.

8 × 3

Madeleine says, "Let's try 12 rows of 2."
The zookeeper is asking a question.
Some of us do not know the answer.
We move back so she will not ask us.

12 × 2

The question is about what is in the sack.
The big, wriggling sack.
We do not want to know.
It looks like we are moving again.

Liam says, "Let's try 24 rows of 1."
A huge python crawls out of the sack
and slithers toward us.
We quickly move farther back.
If we move back any more, we will be
in the street!

24 × 1

Mr. Martin calls, "Show's over! Put your chairs back in the storeroom."
"Okay," we say. "How many rows should we put them in?"